BUILDING WONDERS OF THE WORLD

PATRICIA BAHREE

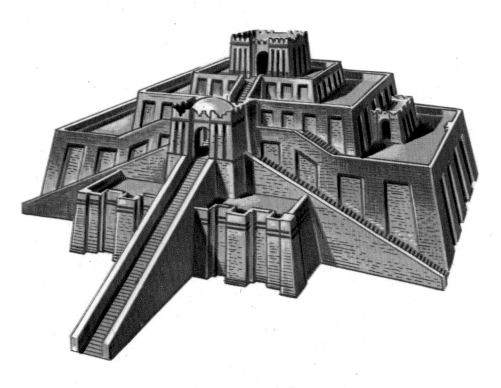

MACDONALD

Editor Susan Simpson
Designer Peter Luff
Illustrated by:
Rob Burns
Dan Escott
Peter North
Ray Turvey
Chris Warner
Barry Salter

The publishers would like to
acknowledge their indebtedness
to Guinness Superlatives Ltd.
(1980 edition) for the confirmation
of certain facts and figures given
in this book.

©Macdonald & Co. 1982

Conceived and produced by
Theorem Publishing Limited

First published in 1982 by
Macdonald & Co. (Publishers) Ltd
Holywell House
Worship Street
London EC2A 2EN

ISBN 0 356 07096 4

Printed and Bound in Great Britain
by Purnell and Sons (Book Production) Ltd.,
Paulton, Bristol

Key to cover

1. The Parthenon is the finest
example of an ancient Greek temple.
Read about its history on page 17.

2. New York, the city of skyscrapers,
is not where you will find the tallest
building in the world. That record is
held by the Sears Tower in Chicago.
See page 12.

3. The pyramids of ancient Egypt
were built to house the mummified
bodies of powerful pharaohs. Many
other civilizations also honour the
dead with lavish tombs. Find out more
on pages 4 and 5.

4. The king who built the castle of
Neuschwanstein was declared mad.
Why? Turn to page 22.

5. The Sydney Opera House is one of
the world's best known landmarks.
Read how it was built on page 27.

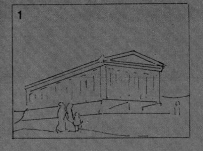

BUILDING WONDERS OF THE WORLD

Civilizations, ancient and modern, have constructed fabulous palaces and tombs, impressive religious and administrative centres, even vast entertainment halls. This book spans thousands of years in the history of civilization, during which time building techniques and materials have undergone enormous changes. Nevertheless, all the buildings described in the following pages are spectacular examples of their kind. Read about wonders of the modern age such as skyscrapers and dams, and discover what steps are being taken to save some of the world's most famous landmarks. At the back of the book you will find useful notes about different architectural features.

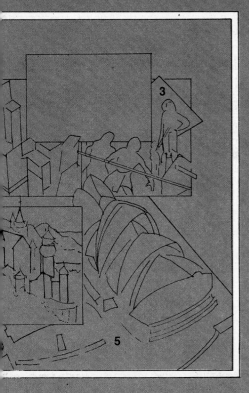

A vision of beauty

Seen during the full moon, the Taj Mahal seems to float like some dream palace. However, it is not a palace at all – but the tomb of the seventeenth-century Indian emperor Shah Jahan and his favourite wife, Mumtaz Mahal.

Shah Jahan had the white marble tomb built for his beautiful wife, and he was later buried by her side. Because the royal couple loved flowers, there are blossoms carved in the marble and flower-patterns made from inlaid

stone. The building is set in a peaceful garden. Shah Jahan followed the religion of Islam. The graceful domes, arches and tall towers, called minarets, are key features of Islamic architecture.

Burial Tombs

The world's great buildings take many shapes and forms, and were built for a number of different purposes. Most were made for people to use and appreciate in this life. But some were built with an eye to the world beyond – as final resting places for the dead.

The pyramids, built to hold the bodies of powerful pharaohs of ancient Egypt, are probably the world's most famous tombs. The Egyptians believed that eternal life after death could be enjoyed only if the body was preserved – so they developed the art of making mummies that would lie in tombs built to last for ever.

Buildings made for the dead may still have a message for the living. They serve to remind us of the great achievements and influences of those who lived before us. And they are also a constant reminder that even the greatest civilizations come to an end.

Images of the dead

Tombs of ordinary people can sometimes be as spectacular as those of kings and queens. The Toraja people of Indonesia bury their dead in graves that have been hewn out of rocky cliffs. A figure of each dead person is placed on a gallery outside the tomb. These eerie images stand like a solemn grey audience of the dead watching over the world of the living.

A tomb in Red Square
Vladimir Lenin, founder of the modern Soviet state, died in 1924. His body was embalmed and placed inside a red granite building in Moscow's Red Square. Today, long queues of visitors file past the glass-covered casket to pay their respects to the great leader.

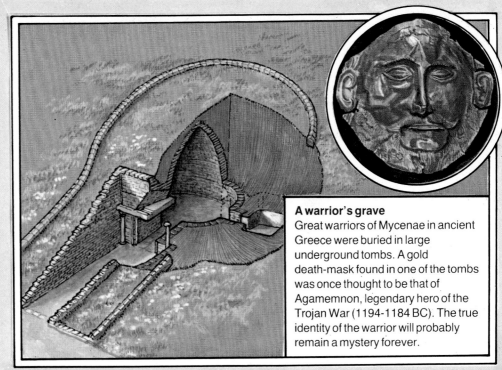

A warrior's grave
Great warriors of Mycenae in ancient Greece were buried in large underground tombs. A gold death-mask found in one of the tombs was once thought to be that of Agamemnon, legendary hero of the Trojan War (1194-1184 BC). The true identity of the warrior will probably remain a mystery forever.

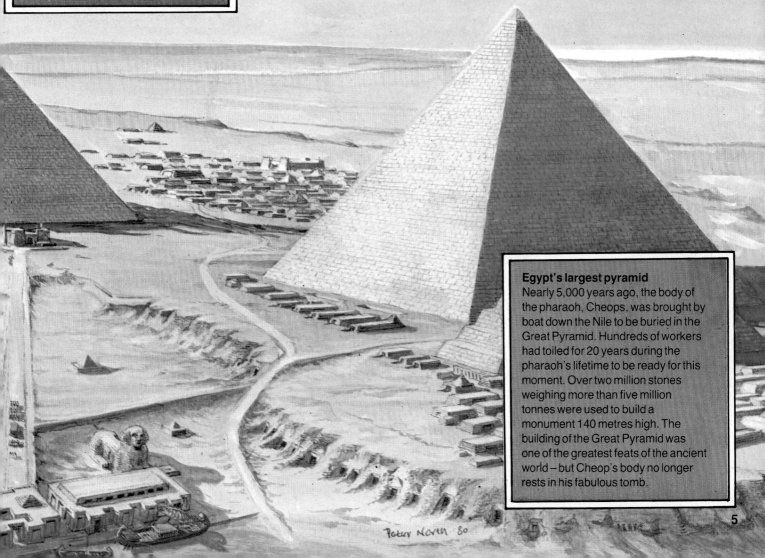

Egypt's largest pyramid
Nearly 5,000 years ago, the body of the pharaoh, Cheops, was brought by boat down the Nile to be buried in the Great Pyramid. Hundreds of workers had toiled for 20 years during the pharaoh's lifetime to be ready for this moment. Over two million stones weighing more than five million tonnes were used to build a monument 140 metres high. The building of the Great Pyramid was one of the greatest feats of the ancient world – but Cheop's body no longer rests in his fabulous tomb.

Splendour from the past

The Qutb Minar, just outside New Delhi, in India, is one of the world's most impressive towers. It was built nearly 800 years ago, during the rule of Qutb-ud-Din Ibak, who was once the Sultan of Delhi. The 73-metre-high tower served as the minaret for a mosque that is now in ruins. It is built of red sandstone and has four balconies.

Dinner in the clouds

If you ever visit Toronto, you can have dinner at the top of one of the world's record-breaking towers. The Canadian National Tower is the world's tallest free-standing structure (it needs no guy-ropes to steady it). It is also the highest tower made out of concrete. The top section of the 553-metre tower had to be lifted into place by a huge helicopter. Above the revolving restaurant is a powerful radio and television aerial.

A tower with a tilt

The Leaning Tower of Pisa is a beautiful building, with eight storeys of graceful rounded arches. But it is famous mainly because, shortly after it was built, the 55-metre-high tower began to lean. Most experts think the soil beneath it shifted. It now tilts six metres to one side.

The world's tallest tower

The tallest structure in the world is the Warszawa radio mast in Plock, Poland. It is 645 metres high and has 15 guy-ropes to steady it. The mast itself is made of tubular galvanized steel. The Warszawa mast has been the world's tallest structure since 1974, but it may not hold the record for much longer. The Soviet Union is planning to build a radio mast that is even higher.

Warszawa radio mast

Eiffel Tower

Reach for the Sky!

The earliest tall buildings were usually constructed for religious or military reasons. In the first instance, a building of great height looks very grand and impressive, and secondly, during a battle, it is easier to spot the enemy from a castle tower or from some other high position. Today, tall structures are built for many other purposes. Skyscrapers have become a familiar sight in modern cities all over the world because they make the best use of the available land. But even skyscrapers are dwarfed by today's towering television and radio masts. Some masts are so tall and slender that they have to be secured with guy-ropes. All high structures will sway in a strong wind to a certain extent, but this is allowed for when they are being built.

The pride of Paris

The workmen building the Eiffel Tower were pioneers of sorts – for this was a revolutionary building. Not only would it be the tallest structure in the world at 302 metres, but also an experiment in the use of the iron frame. Gustav Eiffel designed the tower for the Paris Exhibition of 1889. It was constructed from over 6,000 tonnes of wrought iron. The iron frame led to the modern use of steel frames in skyscrapers.

A symbol of the modern age

The London Post Office Tower has become one of the city's best known landmarks, rising 198 metres into the air. Over 13,000 tonnes of steel, concrete and glass were used in its construction. It had to be tall to provide a clear path above other buildings for the microwaves it sends and receives. Any obstacle in their way could cause distortion. The tower handles telephone, television and radio transmissions.

Early bridges

The earliest bridges were built from whatever material was at hand – stone, tree-trunks or vines. They were only useful for crossing narrow stretches of water. Bridges remained small until people discovered how to build arches.

A large stone or tree-trunk placed across a stream formed the first bridge. Later, flat stone slabs were placed across piles of stone.

The Romans made a great advance in bridge building by using the arch. They built hundreds of stone arch bridges throughout their empire.

The use of metal in bridge building was another great breakthrough. Ironbridge, built in 1779 over the River Severn in England, is the oldest cast-iron bridge still standing.

Spanning the Gap

The world's first bridge was probably built by an inquisitive member of some prehistoric tribe who put a tree-trunk across a stream to find out what was on the other side. Bridge builders have learned a lot since then! Today, they build steel and concrete wonders that span tremendous distances. There are two things bridge designers have to bear in mind – the conditions where the bridge is to be located and the use to which it will be put. There are four main types of bridges. Rigid beam bridges are based on the idea of simply putting a beam or plank across a stream. In a cantilever bridge, two beams are used, one extending from each bank. Suspension bridges consist of steel cables strung between high towers, with a roadway added below. In an arch bridge, one or several arches are the main support. Early arch bridges were made of stone, but as stone is a heavy material, it was eventually replaced by steel.

First in its class

The Humber Bridge in England is the world's longest suspension bridge, with a main span of 1,410 metres. The bridge is made of giant steel cables strung over 163-metre-high concrete towers. Strong wires are used to attach the road deck below. The concrete towers are hollow. Inside are lifts that carry engineers up to the top to carry out cable inspection.

The old coat hanger
Sydney Harbour Bridge in Australia is 48 metres in width – the widest in the world. It has eight lanes of traffic and two overhead railway lines. Built in 1932, the bridge is a familiar part of the Sydney skyline, and is fondly called the 'old coat hanger'.

The longest arch bridge
The longest steel arch bridge in the world is the New River Gorge Bridge in West Virginia in the USA. It has a span of 518 metres. The bridge, completed in 1977, took just three years to build. Sections of the steel arch, weighing up to 86 tonnes, were lifted into place with special cranes.

The ups and downs of London Bridge
The first stone bridge across London's River Thames was lined with shops and houses. It was a sturdy arch bridge, but its wooden piles often cracked and its timber buildings sometimes caught fire. Yet, it was used from 1209 to 1826.

The second London Bridge was completed in 1831. It was a graceful bridge, 306 metres from end to end, with five stone arches. Its designer was John Rennie. After nearly 140 years of service, it met an unusual fate.

John Rennie's bridge was sold to an American for about £1,000,000. Some 10,000 tonnes of granite stone were shipped to the USA and the bridge was rebuilt in Havasu City, Arizona. The third London Bridge, a pre-stressed concrete structure, was opened in 1970.

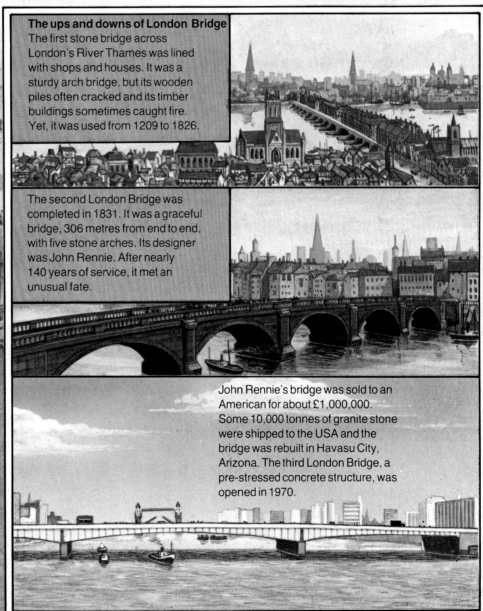

9

The longest road tunnel
The Gotthard road tunnel in Switzerland is 16.3 kilometres long, and is the world's longest road tunnel. It provides a shortcut under the Swiss Alps for people travelling to Italy from such countries as Germany and Belgium. It was opened in 1980 and took ten years to complete. About 4,000 people worked on the project.

An underwater tunnel
Until recently, to get from one part of Hong Kong to the other, you had to take a ferry. But the new Hong Kong Harbour Tunnel makes it possible to drive across in just a few minutes.

Instead of drilling through the earth under the water, giant tubes were made on land, then sunk in a trench in the harbour. A layer of concrete was then poured on top.

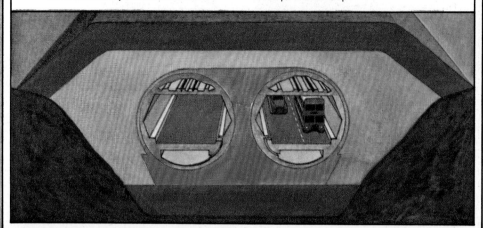

Canals and Tunnels

Canals and tunnels are built for a number of reasons. One of the most important is to provide shortcuts from one place to another. The Suez Canal, for instance, had a tremendous effect on travel and trade. By linking the Mediterranean and Red seas, it made it possible for ships to get from Western Europe to Asia without going all the way around Africa. It cut 7,600 kilometres off the trip from London to Karachi, for example. The Mont Blanc Tunnel, built through the Alps in 1965, shortened the driving distance from Paris to Rome by 200 kilometres.

Major canal and tunnel projects cost enormous amounts of money. They employ huge numbers of workers and machines and may take years to complete. But new discoveries have made the job easier. When Alfred Nobel developed dynamite in 1867, tunnelling entered a new era. Some day laser beams might prove to be an even better way of cutting a path through a mountainside or deep into the ground.

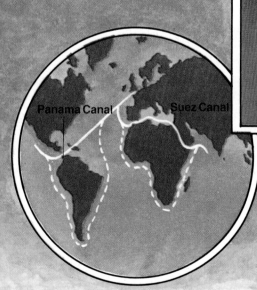

Making the world smaller
The Suez and Panama canals are the world's most important 'shortcuts'. The Suez links Europe with Asia, and the Panama Canal joins the Atlantic and Pacific oceans, cutting out the long trip around South America. Opened in 1914, the Panama Canal is today the world's busiest big-ship canal.

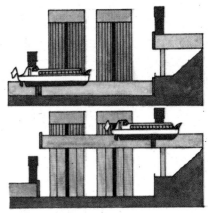

A new kind of lock

The Scharnebeck Ship Lift in Germany solves an old problem in a new way. It takes the place of a lock connecting one water level with another. A ship sailing up the River Elbe into the canal system has to enter a giant tub of water. Gates are closed behind it, then huge electric motors raise the tub up to the level of the canal. The gates are opened on the other side and the ship sails away.

Shortcut to and from the East

The 165-kilometre Suez Canal is the longest canal in the world that can take large ocean-going vessels. It was completed in 1869 – some ten years after work had begun. As many as 8,200 men and 370 camels had been employed on the project. The Suez is a water level canal. This means there is no great difference in the height of the two seas it connects, and so no locks are necessary. Ships can simply sail right through.

A tunnel under the Thames

The Rotherhithe Tunnel, built under the River Thames and completed in 1843 was a brilliant feat of engineering in its day. A device called a tunnelling shield was invented for the job. It was a frame three storeys high. Several frames were placed next to each other so a large number of men could chip away at the stone. The top of the shield supported the roof. Even so, progress was very slow and the tunnel was flooded several times before its completion.

The Empire State Building, at 381 metres tall, is still one of New York's most impressive sights. Built in 1930-31, it was the world's tallest structure for 40 years.

Off to Work

Ancient builders constructed some of the world's greatest tombs, towers and temples, but they rarely built impressive structures for people to work in. Today, some of our grandest and most complicated buildings house important business operations – tall skyscrapers with thousands of offices, gigantic steel mills, huge aircraft factories. These buildings are designed with workers in mind. The surroundings have to be pleasant and there must be plenty of light and fresh air. Perhaps some day you would like to work in a modern record-breaker. Office workers could get a job in the Sears Tower in Chicago – the world's tallest building. A car construction worker could seek employment at the Volkswagen plant in Wolfsburgh, Germany – the world's largest car factory. Or if the food industry sounds more appealing, try working in the world's largest chocolate factory, built by Hershey Foods in Pennsylvania, USA.

A job at the top

On the 6th of March, 1973, the Sears Tower in Chicago became the world's tallest building, topping the World Trade Centre in New York. The building has 110 storeys and is 475 metres high, including its two TV aerials. There are 103 lifts and 18 escalators inside the building taking over 16,000 people to their place of work.

The rush-hour special

Most of the world's great cities have extensive underground railway networks. The London Underground, first opened in 1863, is the oldest. It is also one of the largest, covering 410 kilometres. It carries 500 million passengers a year. The busiest underground system is the New York subway, which carries a billion passengers a year.

A jumbo-sized factory

The Boeing Assembly plant in Everett, Washington, USA, has to be big – since this is where Jumbo jets are made. It is the largest building in the world in terms of space, measuring a total of 5.6 million cubic metres. The Jumbo jets made here are also record-breakers, with room for up to 500 passengers – more than that of any other aircraft. The Jumbo is 70 metres long and has a wing-span of nearly 60 metres.

A steel giant

The world's largest steel-making complex is the Fukuyama Steel Works in Japan, owned by the firm Nippon Kokan. The plant can produce 16 million tonnes of crude steel per year. It covers 1,640 hectares of land – all of which have been reclaimed from the sea.

Temple of peace
One of the largest religious buildings in the world is the Buddhist temple of Sho Hondo, at the foot of Mount Fuji in Japan. It covers nearly 40,000 square metres. The unique roof was modelled on the idea of a crane with wings outspread about to soar into the sky. The temple was opened in 1972, and is dedicated to peace and harmony.

India's towering temples
Most Hindu temples have a tall tower above the main shrine. Sometimes towering gateways lead to the temple. One of the most spectacular is the Madurai temple, built in the 16th century. Its four outer gateways are each over 45 metres high. Madurai is a double temple with two main shrines, one for the god Shiva and the other for his wife. At Madurai, Shiva's wife is called Minakshi, but at other temples she has different names.

A majestic mosque
The Royal Mosque in Isfahan, Iran, has sky-blue domes and towering minarets. It was built in the 17th century. Arabesques – designs formed from curving flowers, leaves and stems – are used for decoration.

A fountain in the courtyard allows worshippers to wash their hands, face and feet as a sign of purity before entering the mosque. Most mosques have a fountain and at least one minaret from which the faithful are called to prayer.

Places of Worship

Religion has inspired many of the world's most beautiful buildings. It has also influenced the way in which they were built. When you enter a Gothic cathedral, its high pointed arches lead your eye heavenward. The altar is the focus of the building, with a large area for community worship. Among the most striking features of mosques are the flowers and geometric shapes used for decoration. These are used because Muhammad, the founder of Islam, believed that there should be no idols and no human or animal figures anywhere in a place of worship. There is no altar – only a niche in the wall showing the direction of the holy city of Mecca, which the faithful face when they pray. In total contrast, a Hindu temple is not designed for group worship. For a Hindu, religion is an individual matter, so there is only a small area in front of the shrine for worshippers to pray alone or in small groups.

A Gothic masterpiece

In Europe, the Middle Ages was the era of cathedrals. Craftsmen's guilds donated money and provided the labour to build beautiful places of worship. Many cathedrals are still religious centres. One of the loveliest is Chartres cathedral in France. It is famous for its superb stained glass windows (inset) and fine sculptured figures. The north spire was added in around 1510. Its ornate Gothic style does not match the simpler style of the southern one, which dates back to 1150.

A striking synagogue

Synagogues are Jewish places of worship. They can be built in any style. The centre of reverence in a synagogue is the Ark of the Covenant, which holds the scrolls of the Torah, or law. Worshippers face towards it when they pray. The world's largest synagogue is the Temple Emanu-El in New York, completed in 1929. Its main sanctuary is 30.7 metres wide and 61.5 metres long, and it can hold 2,500 people.

DAN ESCOTT

The ziggurats of Mesopotamia

The people of Mesopotamia built enormous mounds in each of their cities. At the top was a temple to the city's main god. The 'mound' was called a ziggurat. One of the finest ziggurats was the 21-metre-high structure in the city of Ur. It had several platforms, built one on top of the other. Stone and timber were rare in the area, but there was plenty of clay, so most buildings were made of brick. The ziggurat had a core of mud brick covered by a layer of burnt brick. It was built about 2,125 BC and included the remains of an earlier, much older structure.

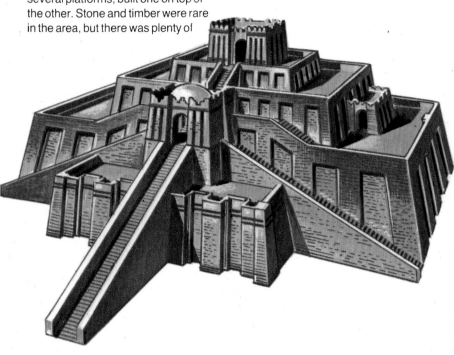

First a temple, now a church

Of all the glorious Roman buildings, the best preserved is a temple, the Pantheon, completed in AD 124. The Pantheon is a round building with a dome that rises to a height of 43 metres and is just over 43 metres in diameter. It was the largest dome of the ancient world. Though built for the Roman gods, the Pantheon is now a Catholic church.

Rescue operation

The Egyptian pharaoh Rameses II is famous for the colossal buildings he erected during his rule. He had two temples carved from the sandstone cliffs at Abu Simbel around 1300 BC. Outside one temple, Rameses had four statues of himself carved – each 20 metres high! In the 1960s, the site was threatened by the building of the Aswan High Dam. The giant lake which was to be created would flood the ancient temples.

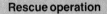

The United Nations led a worldwide effort to save Abu Simbel. Experts decided to move the temple to a spot 65 metres above the new lake. The temples were cut into huge blocks and then lifted by giant cranes. Each of the huge statues weighed over 1,000 tonnes.

Both temples have now been carefully reassembled and are visited by thousands of tourists every year. Moving them cost £17,000,000. It was a colossal effort worthy of Rameses!

DAN ESCOTT

Ancient Temples

Temples were the most important buildings in many ancient cities. They were crowded with people on festival days, when drummers and flute players performed for the gods, and goats and bulls were led to be sacrificed at the temple altar. The finest artists and builders carried out all the construction work on the temples. The results were some of the most beautiful and impressive buildings ever seen. The Mesopotamians raised 20-metre-high mounds with temples on top. The Maya Indians of Central America, who also liked to place their gods high above everyday life, built temple pyramids 60 metres high. Perhaps the most graceful temples of the ancient world were those built by the Greeks, with rows of perfectly balanced columns. Today, these places are no longer used to worship the ancient gods. Instead, they are crowded with tourists, who come to learn a little about life long ago.

A temple for the goddess Athena
In the Greek city of Athens, the most important festival honoured the city's patron goddess, Athena. Long processions wound their way to the Acropolis, or upper city, where her temple, the Parthenon, stood. Made of white marble, the temple was completed in 432 BC and remained in good condition until 1687, when it was damaged by an explosion during fighting. A century later, Lord Elgin, an English diplomat, removed many of the fine statues, which he thought were in danger. Most are now in the British Museum, London.

Temple of the plumed serpent
The city of Chichen Itza in Mexico is now in ruins, but it was once a thriving centre of the Maya Indians, and later of the Toltecs. The most impressive building is a temple, built on top of a pyramid some 60 metres high and reached by four great stairways. The temple, built at the end of the 12th century, was dedicated to Kukulcan, the plumed serpent god.

Famous Cities

More people live in cities now than ever before – over a third of the world's population. Some cities are quite new, planned and built in the 20th century. Others are ancient and have grown and changed haphazardly over the centuries. Local conditions have influenced both the style of buildings in cities and the materials used. Some cities are built mainly of wood, others of brick or stone. Some are marked by domes, others by spires. A few cities, such as Paris, have instantly recognizable skylines. In recent years, however, the world's cities have begun to look more alike. The tall skyscrapers of Nairobi are very much like those of Tokyo or New York. In fact, the modern style of building is sometimes called the International style, since it is used in cities all over the world.

The most crowded
Tokyo has more people than any other city – over 11 million of them. It is Japan's capital as well as its industrial, financial and cultural centre. Tokyo has many modern buildings, since many of its old ones were destroyed either in the great earthquake of 1923, or 20 years later, in the bombing raids of World War II.

On top of the world

One of the world's highest cities is Lhasa, the capital of Tibet which is now a part of China. Until recent times, getting to Lhasa – which is 3,600 metres above sea level – usually meant a slow journey across the Himalaya Mountains. Today, there are paved roads and an airport. Lhasa has many temples and monasteries for it has been a centre of Buddhist religion for centuries. One of its most beautiful buildings is the Potala, once the home of the Dalai Lama, who was the head of the church and ruler of Tibet.

Ancient biblical city

Experts think Jericho was the world's first city, dating back to 8,000 BC. It was surrounded by great walls. The Bible tells how Joshua's army won the battle of Jericho – trumpets were sounded and the walls tumbled down.

Skyscraper city

New York is one of the world's tallest cities, with streets like deep canyons between towering skyscrapers. As the city's importance grew, the island of Manhattan – its centre – became crowded, so the only way left to go was up.

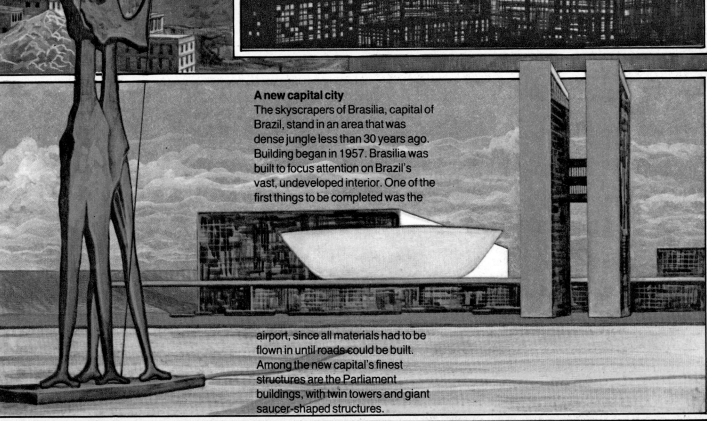

A new capital city

The skyscrapers of Brasilia, capital of Brazil, stand in an area that was dense jungle less than 30 years ago. Building began in 1957. Brasilia was built to focus attention on Brazil's vast, undeveloped interior. One of the first things to be completed was the airport, since all materials had to be flown in until roads could be built. Among the new capital's finest structures are the Parliament buildings, with twin towers and giant saucer-shaped structures.

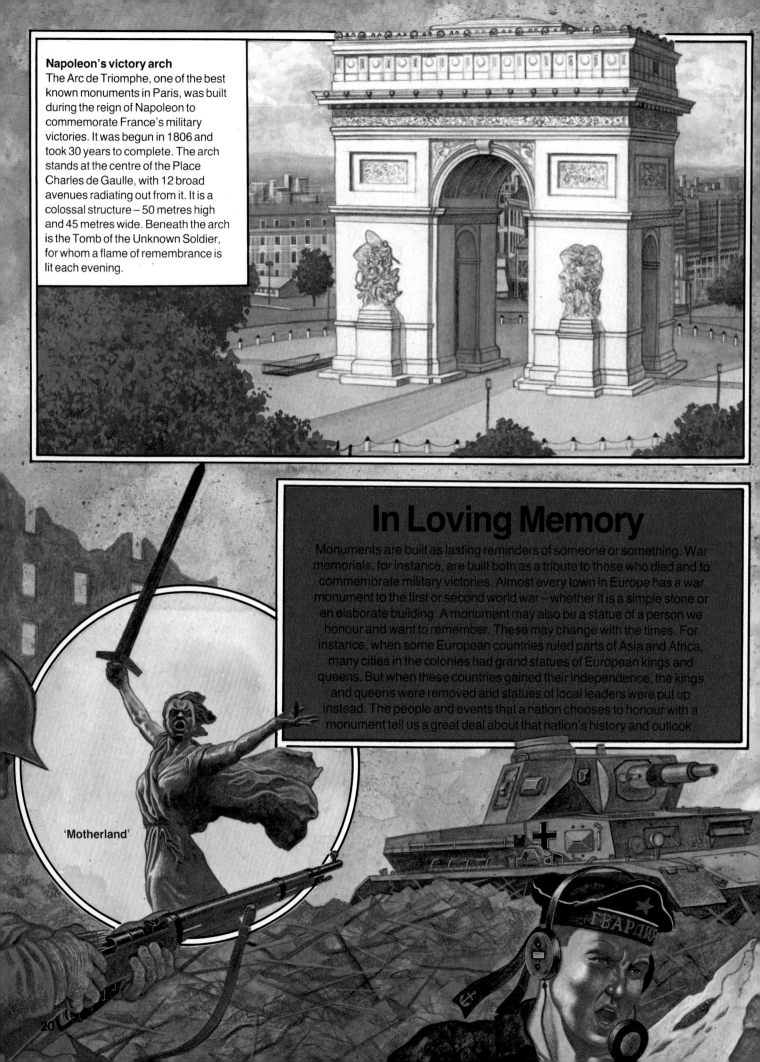

Napoleon's victory arch

The Arc de Triomphe, one of the best known monuments in Paris, was built during the reign of Napoleon to commemorate France's military victories. It was begun in 1806 and took 30 years to complete. The arch stands at the centre of the Place Charles de Gaulle, with 12 broad avenues radiating out from it. It is a colossal structure – 50 metres high and 45 metres wide. Beneath the arch is the Tomb of the Unknown Soldier, for whom a flame of remembrance is lit each evening.

'Motherland'

In Loving Memory

Monuments are built as lasting reminders of someone or something. War memorials, for instance, are built both as a tribute to those who died and to commemorate military victories. Almost every town in Europe has a war monument to the first or second world war – whether it is a simple stone or an elaborate building. A monument may also be a statue of a person we honour and want to remember. These may change with the times. For instance, when some European countries ruled parts of Asia and Africa, many cities in the colonies had grand statues of European kings and queens. But when these countries gained their independence, the kings and queens were removed and statues of local leaders were put up instead. The people and events that a nation chooses to honour with a monument tell us a great deal about that nation's history and outlook.

Great 'heads' of state
In a gigantic monument to democracy, the heads of four American presidents have been carved in the granite face of Mount Rushmore, in South Dakota. George Washington, Thomas Jefferson, Theodore Roosevelt and Abraham Lincoln were chosen for their roles in founding, shaping and strengthening the country. Each head measures 18 metres from chin to forehead. The carving was begun in 1927, and took 14 years to complete.

Gateway to the American West
The world's tallest monument is the stainless steel Gateway Arch, built beside the Mississippi River in St. Louis, Missouri, USA. It commemorates the move westward in the early 1800s, when St. Louis was the last city many pioneers passed through. The arch, completed in 1965, is 192 metres high and has lifts up to the top.

A statue for Stalingrad
The world's tallest statue stands on Marnayev Hill outside Volgograd (previously Stalingrad) in the USSR. It is a female figure made of pre-stressed concrete, called 'Motherland', which measures 82 metres from base to sword tip. The figure is a memorial to the Soviet victory in the Battle of Stalingrad during World War II. The battle lasted from August 1942 to February 1943. The Soviet victory over the German army marked a turning point in the war.

Pillars of victory
The Romans sometimes erected tall columns to honour important victories. One of the finest is Trajan's column, built around AD113 and showing scenes of the emperor's victories. The column, made entirely of marble, is 35 metres high and has over 2,500 human figures carved on it, many involved in dramatic land and sea battles. The emperor Trajan is buried in a tomb beneath the column.

Safe from Attack

Castles served two main purposes – they were strongholds in times of war and they were also the homes of kings or nobles, their families and many of their soldiers. Many castles were built in Europe during the Middle Ages, largely because the power of the kings was always under threat. Every noble was also required to defend his own territory. One of the most important parts of the castle was the keep – a tower large enough for the noble's family and garrison to live in during attacks. Many castles had several courtyards, or baileys, enclosed by a high wall. The wall was sometimes surrounded by a moat that could only be crossed by a drawbridge. Specially shaped holes in the wall allowed archers to fire their bows from safety. There were also openings at several points in the wall so that stones or boiling water could be dropped on the heads of attackers.

A crusader castle
Krak des Chevaliers in modern-day Syria is one of the best preserved castles dating from the Crusades. The Knights of St. John captured it in 1142 and rebuilt it. Then in 1271 it fell to the Turkish sultan, Baibar. The castle had enough living space for 2,000 men.

'Mad' Ludwig's dream castle
By the time Ludwig II of Bavaria came to the throne in the late 19th century, the age of knights and castles was over. But Ludwig loved dreaming of bygone days and built himself a storybook castle. He neglected the government and spent so much time and money building his fantastic castles and palaces that his ministers had him declared mad and removed from power.

A bloody past
The Tower of London has served both as a castle and a prison. The oldest part is the keep, which was started soon after 1066 by William the Conqueror. Famous prisoners kept in the Tower in later times include the young princes Edward V and his brother Richard, who were brought to the Tower in 1483 and never seen again; and two of the six wives of Henry VIII, who were kept in the Tower before their heads were chopped off.

A walled city

During the Middle Ages in Europe, whole towns were sometimes fortified. Carcassonne in France, built mainly in the 13th century, is surrounded by two walls, with over 50 watch-towers, and also by a moat.

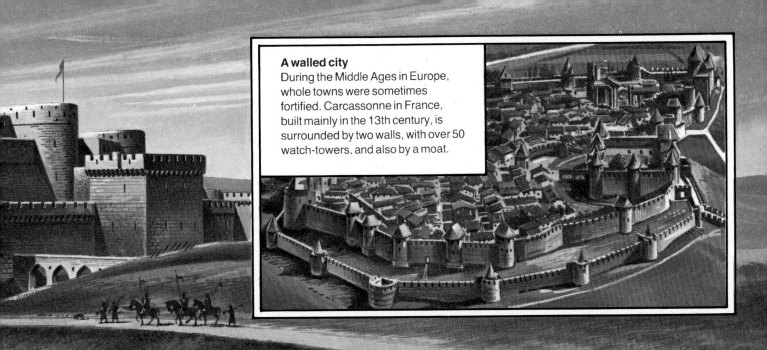

Plan of Himeji castle

A fort for India's emperors

The Red Fort in Delhi gets its name from the high red sandstone wall that surrounds it. There are two main gates, of which the southern one was used for royal processions. Inside the walls are a number of buildings, made mainly of white marble, and set among beautiful gardens. The fort was built around 1640 by Shah Jahan, creator of the Taj Mahal.

Castle of the White Heron

During the 16th and 17th centuries, when Japan was torn by civil war, nobles built themselves fortified castles. One of the finest is Himeji castle, surrounded by a wall, a moat, and several earthen ramparts. The keep is several storeys high with layers of sloping roofs. From a distance, it looks like a giant white bird, which is why it is popularly called the Castle of the White Heron.

23

An Islamic masterpiece
The Alhambra is one of the world's loveliest palaces. It is located in the Spanish town of Granada and was built mainly in the 14th century by the Muslim rulers of Spain. Parts of it were reserved for royalty, while other areas – including the Hall of Judgement shown above – were used for public functions.

Fit for a King

The castles built in Europe during the Middle Ages were not very comfortable to live in. The windows were small – both for defence reasons and to keep the cold winds out. There was no window glass, so wooden shutters were used, but these cut out the light as well as the draughts. The only heat came from fireplaces. The keep was often not only cold and dark, but also crowded – with nobles and soldiers all living under one roof. To build a palace that was truly fit for a king, a ruler needed to be secure enough to concentrate on beauty rather than defence. A large and steady income was also necessary. When these conditions were met, royalty could live in breathtaking luxury – like the elaborately decorated Alhambra in Spain or the elegant Palace of Versailles in France.

Gondolas at the palace door
Venice, in northern Italy, was once a great trading power. It was ruled by an elected official called the Doge, who lived in the Doge's Palace which was constructed mainly in the 14th century and was sited right on the edge of the lagoon. The two lower floors have lovely open hallways lined with arches that overlook the water. The inside is equally beautiful, with grand staircases, rich decoration, and paintings by Italian masters.

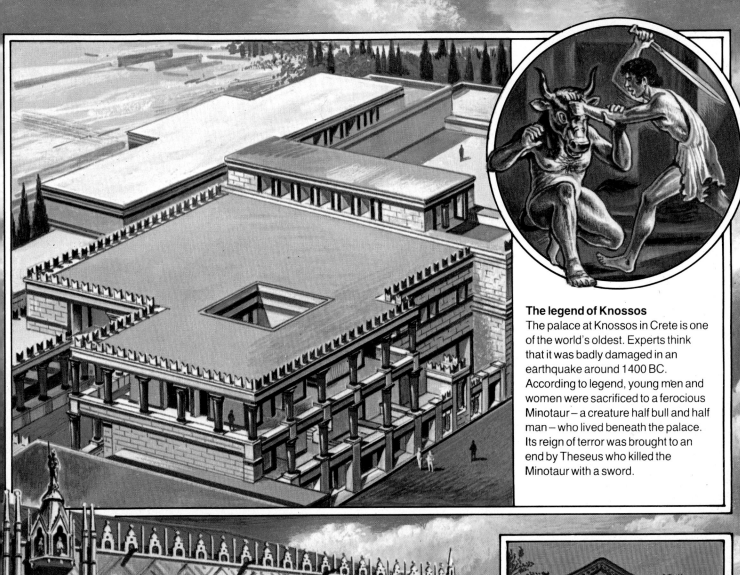

The legend of Knossos
The palace at Knossos in Crete is one of the world's oldest. Experts think that it was badly damaged in an earthquake around 1400 BC. According to legend, young men and women were sacrificed to a ferocious Minotaur – a creature half bull and half man – who lived beneath the palace. Its reign of terror was brought to an end by Theseus who killed the Minotaur with a sword.

The Forbidden City
The Imperial Palace in Peking was built mainly by the emperor Yung Lo in the 15th century. It is said that it was completed in just five years – by employing a million workers! The palace area, which has several ornate buildings, was called the Forbidden City, since no ordinary person could enter it.

DAN ESCOTT

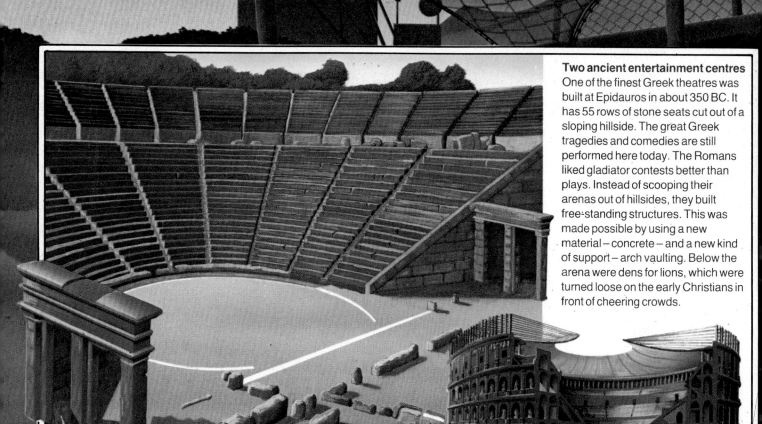

Entertainment for All

Places of entertainment rank among the world's largest and most spectacular buildings. Equally impressive structures were also known in ancient times. As early as 500 BC, the Greeks were building theatres by hollowing a space out of a hillside. Stone seats were arranged in a horseshoe shape round a circular stage and all the performances took place in the open air. The Romans built great amphitheatres for holding gladiator contests and wild animal shows. The largest is the Colosseum in Rome, which covers two hectares and had seats for about 50,000 people. Today, many cities have stadia that are even more enormous than the Colosseum. The biggest is the Strahov Stadium in Prague, Czechoslovakia, which can hold 240,000 spectators. The largest indoor stadium is the Superdome in Louisiana in the USA, where over 76,000 fans can watch a football game.

The home of Mickey Mouse
The world's largest amusement resort is Disney World, in Florida in the USA. It was built in 1971 and covers 11,000 hectares. Both Disney World and Disneyland in California were inspired by Walt Disney, the creator of cartoon characters such as Mickey Mouse and Donald Duck. Several million people visit each park every year.

Two ancient entertainment centres
One of the finest Greek theatres was built at Epidauros in about 350 BC. It has 55 rows of stone seats cut out of a sloping hillside. The great Greek tragedies and comedies are still performed here today. The Romans liked gladiator contests better than plays. Instead of scooping their arenas out of hillsides, they built free-standing structures. This was made possible by using a new material – concrete – and a new kind of support – arch vaulting. Below the arena were dens for lions, which were turned loose on the early Christians in front of cheering crowds.

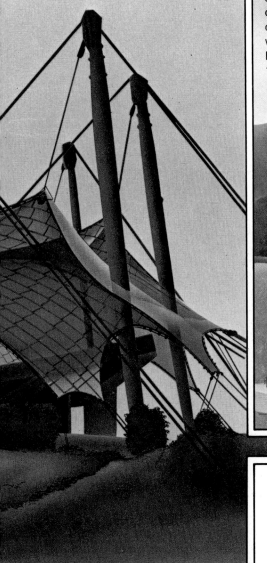

A shape to fit the setting

The spectacular Sydney Opera House in Australia was designed with a sail-like roof, to resemble the sail boats in the harbour. Building the roof proved difficult. Pre-cast concrete sections were lifted into place by cranes and reinforced with steel cables. The roof was then covered with over a million tiles. The Opera House, which opened in 1973, took 14 years to build.

The inside-out building

The Pompidou Arts Centre in Paris is not just famous for its works of art and entertainment programmes. The building itself is also one of the most extraordinary in the world. It is, in a sense, built inside out. All of the steel supports usually covered by walls are on the outside, as well as lifts, stairs, pipes and ducts. You can barely see the glass walls, which are under the steel skeleton. The building was completed in 1977, but its unusual appearance still leaves some visitors asking when it's finally going to be finished.

A giant tent

When the Olympic Games were held in Munich in 1972, a new kind of stadium was built for the event. Its roof is made of thousands of clear plastic sheets, held together with steel strips. Cables attach the plastic roof to masts 80 metres tall, rather like a giant tent. This new-style roof has proved to be a success. It keeps off the rain, but lets in the light, and there are no pillars inside to spoil the view.

Oil from beneath the sea

The world's largest oil platform is the Ninian Central Platform in the North Sea. Building it was a mammoth task. The concrete base was first built in dry dock and then floated out to sea. It weighed more than 100,000 tonnes. Once at sea, the 155-metre concrete tower was built. Then the giant steel deck was added. Steel for the deck alone weighed more than 6,000 tonnes. Oil rigs are located on the platform, with pipes in the core of the tower for oil to pass through.

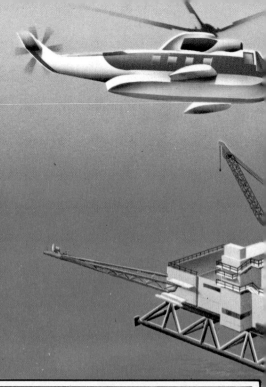

A light to guide ships

Lighthouses are built at the entrances to ports, and at spots that might be dangerous for ships. The earliest lighthouse, the Pharos of Alexandria, was about 100 metres high. Its light, made by wood fires and reflectors, could be seen for over 50 kilometres. It was destroyed by an earthquake in 1375. The tallest lighthouse today is a steel tower, 106 metres high, in Japan.

Specialized Structures

There are a great many structures dotted around the world that are not necessarily noted for their beauty, but which are remarkable building achievements nevertheless. One example from the ancient world is the Great Wall of China. Although it was built over 2,000 years ago, it is still by far the world's longest wall. Another ancient marvel is Stonehenge, in Great Britain. This gigantic stone circle may have been a prehistoric observatory. Its giant upright stones weigh about 25 tonnes each and they are capped by horizontal stones weighing seven tonnes. There are, of course, building wonders of the modern world, too. One of the greatest engineering triumphs of recent years must be the giant oil and gas production platforms out in the North Sea. These steel and concrete monsters have a very complicated structure – nothing like them has ever been built before.

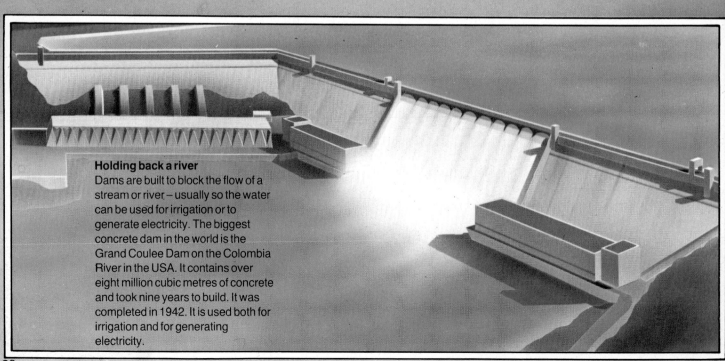

Holding back a river

Dams are built to block the flow of a stream or river – usually so the water can be used for irrigation or to generate electricity. The biggest concrete dam in the world is the Grand Coulee Dam on the Colombia River in the USA. It contains over eight million cubic metres of concrete and took nine years to build. It was completed in 1942. It is used both for irrigation and for generating electricity.

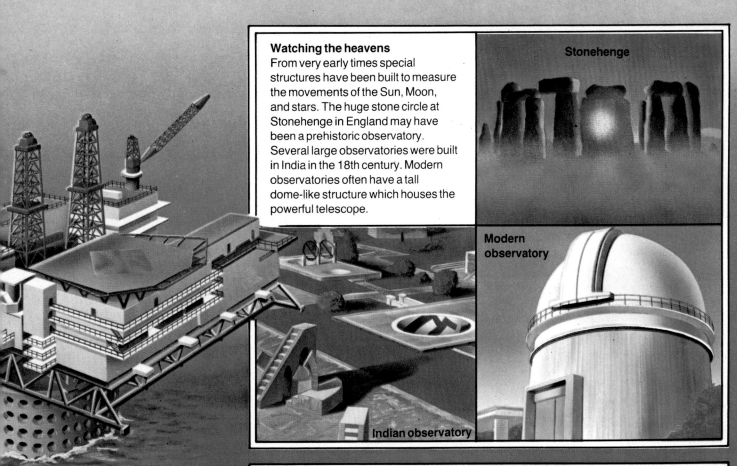

Watching the heavens

From very early times special structures have been built to measure the movements of the Sun, Moon, and stars. The huge stone circle at Stonehenge in England may have been a prehistoric observatory. Several large observatories were built in India in the 18th century. Modern observatories often have a tall dome-like structure which houses the powerful telescope.

Stonehenge

Modern observatory

Indian observatory

Towers for power stations

In many power stations, huge amounts of water are heated to make steam, which is used to drive electricity generators. The water must then be cooled, so giant towers have been designed to do the job. The sloping shape of the concrete towers speeds the air flow to give better cooling.

Keeping out the enemy

The Chinese emperor Shih Huang Ti built the Great Wall of China in the 3rd century BC, to keep roving tribes from raiding his empire. About half the 2,260-kilometre wall was built during his reign, and about a third of the able-bodied men in his empire worked on it. The wall is between six and nine metres high, and is so long that the American astronauts reported they could see it from the moon as a distinct line!

Some useful words

Arch The curved support over an opening. A true arch is formed of wedge-shaped bricks or blocks of stone held together by mutual pressure and supported only at the sides. (see below).

Balcony A platform extending from a building, usually with a rail or low wall around it and a door opening onto it.

Belfry The upper room in a tower where bells are hung. Sometimes the tower itself is called a belfry.

Buttress Brick or masonry built against a wall to give added strength. A *flying buttress* is an arch or half-arch built against a wall to take the thrust of the roof or vaulting.

Capital The crowning feature at the top of a column (see below).

Column A vertical support, usually with three parts: the *base, shaft* and *capital*. The ancient Greeks had three different styles of column. The *Doric* column has no base and the capital is plain. The *Ionic* column is usually thinner and lighter with a scroll or spiral decoration on the capital. The *Corinthian* has a capital decorated with leaves plus the scroll or spiral. A column in the form of a female figure is called a *caryatid*.

Concrete A mixture of water, sand, stone and a binder, such as cement. The Romans were the first to use concrete. *Reinforced concrete,* widely used today, has steel rods or mesh running through it to strengthen it. *Precast concrete* is also often used for modern buildings. Ready-made sections are brought from the factory and then simply placed in position.

Crypt The space under a building. In churches generally used for burial in early times.

Curtain wall A wall which does not carry the weight of the building, but is simply hung on the frame like a curtain.

Dome A rounded roof, placed like an upturned cup over a building.

Facade The front or face of a building.

Fluting Shallow grooves running vertically on the shaft of a column or other surface.

Gable Triangular part of a wall, between the two sloping sides of a roof.

Gargoyle A water spout to throw off water from the roof, usually carved in the shape of a strange face.

Keystone The central stone of an arch, often richly carved.

Mouldings The decorative shapes given to bands standing out from the rest of a wall (see below).

Parapet A low wall protecting a place where there is a sudden drop, for instance at the edge of a bridge.

Rose window A large, round window, often over the main entrance in a Gothic cathedral.

Spire The tall, tapering section at the top of a tower.

Tracery Ornamental pattern-work filling the top of a window.

Turret A very small, slender tower, often with stairs inside.

Vault An arched ceiling or roof.

Window An opening made in a wall for light or ventilation (see below).

Arches

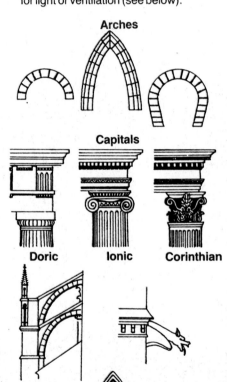

Capitals

Doric   Ionic   Corinthian

Buttress

Windows

Things to do

Are there any famous buildings near your home? If so, you might want to find out more about them. If you live in a big city, you'll find plenty of guide books to help you. If not, your town may have an historical society that could tell you which local buildings are being preserved and why. Libraries can often help, too. For instance, your library may have a map showing which buildings were standing 100 years ago. Or it may have old pictures of your city or town.

Books to read

If you would like to find out more about the world's great buildings, you might read some of the following books:

John H. Stephens. *The Guinness Book of Structures*. Guinness Superlatives Ltd.

Helen and Richard Leacroft have written several books on early buildings. These include *The Buildings of Ancient Egypt, The Buildings of Ancient Greece* and *The Buildings of Early Islam*. Hodder and Stoughton, and Addison-Wesley Publishing Co.

Alun Lewis. *Super Structures*. Woodpecker Books.

David Macauley has written and illustrated a number of books on buildings including *Castle, Pyramid, Cathedral,* and *City*. Collins.

Anne and Scott MacGregor have produced several project books, including *Skyscraper* and *Bridges*. Pepper Press.

The Old and the New

If you have enjoyed reading about the world's great buildings, you might want to find out more about what is being done to preserve them. Some sites you could investigate include the Parthenon in Greece, the Sphinx in Egypt, the Ajanta caves in India, and the great Buddhist monument of Borobudur in Java, which is shown on this page. At Borobudur a new reinforced concrete foundation is being built. In the process, over a million stone blocks will have to be removed, classified, cleaned and put back in the right place. Work is also underway to solve a number of problems facing the city of Venice. The problems and some solutions are described below.

Of course, not all old buildings can be saved. If they were, there would be no room for bold, modern structures that combine good design with excellent living facilities. Probably the best solution is to blend the best of the old with the new.

Saving a sinking city

Venice is one of the world's most beautiful cities, but its treasures of art and architecture are being threatened. The three major problems are flooding at times of high tide, air pollution, and the fact that the city is sinking into the soft silt on which it is built, at a rate of 30 centimetres per year. A mammoth project has been launched to save Venice. Gigantic barriers are being planned to control flood waters, air pollution laws are being put into force, and limits have been placed on the amount of water that can be pumped from underground, since pumping the water is one of the reasons why Venice has been sinking.

Famous architects and engineers

Buildings and other structures are designed by architects and engineers. Their plans are drawn up for builders to follow, though the architect or engineer supervises the work until the structure is completed. A few of the world's great architects and engineers are described below.

Gianlorenzo Bernini (1598-1680), one of Italy's many great architects, designed some of the finest buildings in Rome. Bernini was not only an architect, but also a sculptor, painter and poet. His style of building was generally grand and luxurious, with sweeping curves and elaborate decoration.

Le Corbusier (1887-1966) was one of the most important architects of the present century. He pioneered the smooth glass and metal style in which many skyscrapers are built today. Le Corbusier was born in Switzerland, but the buildings which he designed are in many countries. He helped to create the United Nations Building in New York, planned the new city of Chandigarh in India and designed the Museum of Modern Art in Tokyo, among many other buildings.

Gustave Eiffel (1832-1923), a French engineer, is famous mainly for designing the Eiffel Tower, which is named after him. He also built several iron bridges and was the engineer for the Statue of Liberty, in New York, which has an interior iron frame.

Oscar Niemeyer (b. 1907) of Brazil, was the chief architect of the group that planned the new capital city, Brasilia. His buildings include the president's palace, the houses of parliament and the cathedral of Brasilia.

Sir Christopher Wren (1632-1723) was one of Britain's greatest architects. After the great Fire of London in 1666, Wren was given a remarkable opportunity. He was put in charge of rebuilding the city. His buildings include 51 churches designed for the city – and his masterpiece, St. Paul's Cathedral.

Frank Lloyd Wright (1869-1959) is the United States' most famous architect. He designed homes, churches, office buildings and factories. Wright's designs are fresh and original – and sometimes daringly unusual. One of his most striking buildings is the Guggenheim Museum in New York, built as a spiral ramp along which paintings are hung.

Index